# Introd

Scoubidous are great fun. You [...] fashion jewellery. Bracelets are [...] necklaces are just as easy.

Scoubidous are so versatile that you can make figures, brooches, fridge magnets even things for your pencil case and hair.

One of the nice things about crafting with scoubidous is that you can start making things with only scoubi strands and scissors. But, if you start to add beads, pom poms, pipe cleaners and eyes etc, the possibilities become as endless as your imagination.

The skills you require are as advanced or as simple as you want to make them. This book is a comprehensive instruction manual but it also features projects where no knotting skills are needed. So even younger children can join in the fun and enjoy making things.

Remember though that scoubidous should not be given to very young children, especially under 3's as there is a risk of strangulation and small components can cause choking.

## Lets get started . . . . . . . . . . . .

This book is divided into 3 sections:

The pink section      is the instruction section.

The lavender section      is the no knotting project section

The green section      is the knotted project section

# Contents

## Skills Section

## No knotting section

# Knotted project section

## Getting started

Scoubidous are as simple or as complicated as you choose to make them. The only equipment you definitely need are scoubidou strands and scissors. BUT you will not be able to stop there!

You will quickly want to start including accessories to widen your scope for even more fantastic projects.

Once you have mastered the basics you can start to make all sorts of jewellery. Useful accessories to make jewellery would typically include, bracelet and necklace jump rings and clasps, earring wires or clips, hair clips and brooch backs.

For key rings and zip pulls you will need split rings in differing sizes. You may like to use magnets or even pens!

Once you have mastered the basics you can start to make scoubi 'models'. It is essential to use wire if you want to shape your project into a particular style and wire is often very useful for completing models and projects.

Apart from scoubis and wire you can incorporate beads, joggle eyes, pom poms, felt, feathers or pipe cleaners etc. The list is as endless as your imagination.

Don't forget, you do not have to go out and buy everything. As an example, you can often recycle beads from old and broken necklaces or bracelets.

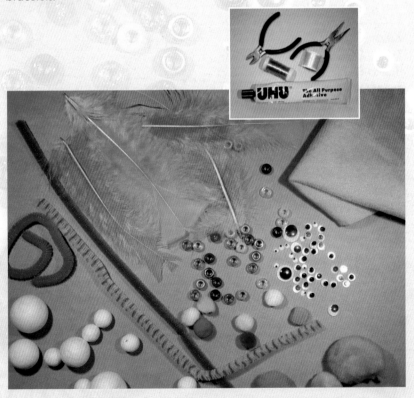

## Start Knots 1 & 2

### Knot 1

Take 4 strands and tie them together at the top.
Spread them out as shown in the picture.

### Knot 2

Take 2 strands and fold them in
half to find the centre point. Tie a
knot leaving loops at the top, which
are large enough for you to attach
your accessories.

### Variation

Make a loop with just one strand and tie the second strand as shown.

This is useful when working on
spiral or plait stitch. It is also
useful for some key rings, zip pulls
or scoubis for your bike.

## Start Knots 1 & 2

To start, using knot 1 and 2.
Using the purple strand, make a loop facing forwards.

With the blue strand, make a loop by taking the strand behind. You should now have 2 loops, one purple and one blue.

Thread the right hand white strand through the purple loop.

And then the pink strand through the blue loop. Pull all strands firmly but carefully using equal tension.

You should end up with a base that looks like the picture opposite.

You can now choose which stitch to use for your first project.

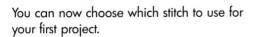

## Start Knots

### Knot 3

Take 2 strands and fold them in half to find the centre, position the centres as shown in the photograph

Holding strands between your thumb and index finger make one top loop

And then another below

Next, thread the right hand strand through the top loop

And then the left hand strand through the bottom loop

Still holding the strands between your thumb and index finger, carefully pull strands to form your base knot.

Once you have the right shape in place, pull the strands firmly to form a secure base for your next stitches.

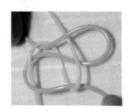

The pink section

## The Square Knot

The square knot is usually the first stitch to master.  It is basically the same process as the starting knot – you just keep repeating the steps. You must make sure that you start with the start base and when you have finished a stitch you will still have this shape.  So,

Still holding the starting knot between your thumb and index finger, make a top loop, and then a bottom loop. Thread the right hand strand through the top loop and the left hand strand through the bottom loop. Carefully pull all stitches to form the knot and then go back and tighten stitches.

**Note:** on the second row the process is reversed, so the top loop is on the right and the left strand is threaded through. The bottom loop is on the left and the right hand strand is threaded through.

### TIPS

- *If you make very tight knots be careful not to snap the strands.*

- *If you make loose knots, your scoubi will grow faster but will have a different overall look.*

- *Quite tight looks neat and is probably the tension you are aiming for. It is the best method when you need to reinforce your scoubi.*

- *Handcream, butter, food  etc. do not mix very well with scoubis. It makes them impossible to work because they become very slippery and will not stay in a knot.*

If you are having difficulty understanding the instructions and illustrations, why not persuade an adult to learn and then show you how to do it!

## The Round Knot

The round scoubi knot is a variation on the square knot but gives a different effect. You must start with the illustrated base starting stitch. Thereafter you work the strands diagonally.

Still holding the starting knot between your thumb and index finger make a diagonal loop on the top.

And then a second diagonal loop on the bottom.

Thread the right hand strand through the top loop.

And then thread the left hand strand through the bottom loop.

Still holding the strands between your thumb and index finger, carefully pull strands to form the now familiar base.

Once you have the right shape in place, tighten the strands firmly to form the base for your next knotting stitches.

Keep repeating this process until you reach the desired length.

# The Triangular Scoubi

To start, use knot 1 and open out.

### Stitch One
Make a loop with the white strand and place thread over the black strand.

Next, make another loop with the black strand and pass over the yellow strand. Thread the yellow strand through the first white loop.

Pull carefully until the stitch is neat and reasonably tight. You should have a triangular shape.

### Stitch Two
Is worked in exactly the same way but starts with the yellow strand.

### Stitch Three
Starts with the black strand.

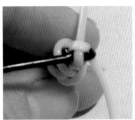

# How to finish

There are several ways to complete or finish off your scoubi, this book shows you three different ways.

## Method 1

The easiest of all, and quite reliable, is to pull the last stitch tightly and snip close to the ends.

## Method 2

If you want to be really sure your last stitch will hold, use a drop of strong glue on the last stitch before cutting.

### TIP

It is often better to pull the last stitch tight and leave overnight before snipping the ends.  This encourages your scoubi to 'set' and generally prevents the last stitch unravelling.

## Method 3

Take 2 diagonal strands and tie together tightly. Trim ends closely. Take the remaining 2 strands, again tie tightly and trim closely.

# The Completion Knot

## Method 4

Make the last stitch loosely.

Next, start with any strand and move it around the next strand to the left. Push this strand under that stitch until it comes through the middle.

Turn your scoubi 90 degrees so as the next strand is in front of you and repeat the last step.

Continue with the last two strands, remember to keep turning. All strands should be in the middle of the scoubi.

Carefully pull all the strands tight through the middle so as the bottom stitch is secure and neat.

Cut remaining strands.

## Reinforcing and Wiring

By reinforcing a strand or scoubi you can increase the flexibility and widen the range of projects you can make. It is much easier to shape your creation when it is wired.

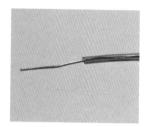

## Using knot 3

When using knot 3 you can use one of two methods.

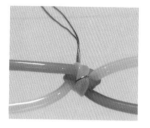

The more secure is to attach a length of wire, which has been folded in half, on the bottom strand whilst starting. Keep the wire central. or insert after the base stitch is completed.

Remember to work around the wire as you knot keeping it hidden in the middle.

Cut the ends closely and bend into the shape you require.

# Lengthening Strands

You will find that some projects need longer strands. Don't worry because it is not difficult to add strands to lengthen whilst working. Just a little patience and practise is all it takes.

Firstly, take a new strand and find its centre. Place this new strand over the base stitch at its central point.

Holding the new strand in place, work another stitch, using existing threads, over the new strand. (Try to ignore the strand you are not working with.) Pull the stitch very tightly to disguise the new join as much as possible and to keep it neat.

Trim the unneeded threads closely to the body of your scoubi.

Work at least two more complete stitches using all strands to secure more firmly before repeating the procedure for the other strands.

# The Spiral Knot

The spiral is easiest to start using knot 2.

This stitch will use the outside strands a lot faster than the supporting middle strands. Therefore, you will usually have to use strands double the length for the outside.

## Stitch One

After tying your start knot, lay your 4 strands flat.

Take the outside right blue strand over the middle two strands but underneath the outside left strand.

- You will have a sort of blue loop.

Next, take the outside left strand and thread behind the middle strands bringing it through the blue loop.

Pull carefully until the stitch is neat and reasonably tight.

## Stitch Two

Is exactly the same as stitch one. The spiral always starts with the outside right hand strand.

Make sure to remember to thread the outside right strand in front of the middle two strands and the left hand strand behind.

As this stitch grows, the stitches will turn around the middle strands creating a spiral effect.

## Variation

For another effect try working two strands for the outside strands.

## The Plait

This knot has a similar construction to the spiral but ends up flat. This makes it very comfortable for bracelets and necklaces.

Like the spiral, this stitch will use the outside strands a lot faster than the supporting middle strands. Therefore, you will usually have to use strands double the length for the outside.

The only difference starts with the second stitch.

### Stitch One

See page 14, the spiral knot, and follow the directions.

### Stitch Two

Follows the same principle but, you must remember to start each new stitch from the opposite side to the last.

So, take the outside left pink strand over the middle two strands but behind the pink strand on the opposite right hand side.

Pull tight, but evenly.

### Stitch Three
Is the same as stitch one.

### Stitch Four
Is the same as stitch two.

### Completion
Tie a knot on the back of the work and pull tightly.  Trim closely.

### Variation
For another effect try working two strands for the outside strands.

# The 6 Stranded Scoubi

This stitch uses the same principles as the triangular scoubi.  It is also an excellent technique to use with just 4 strands, 8 strands or even more!

To start, take 6 strands and tie them together using knot 1 and open out.

Make a loop with the white strand placing the thread over the black strand.

Next, make another loop with the black thread and place over the grey.

Place the grey over the yellow,

the yellow over the green, and the green over the pink. Finally the pink strand threads through the original starting white loop.

Slowly pull down on all the strands to loosely tighten.

Go back and individually tighten each strand to look like the picture.

Repeat the steps until you reach the desired length. You need to start the next stitch with the pink strand, the third with the black etc.

## The 8 Stranded Rectangular Scoubi

Find the centres of the 3 strands and tie them together with a 4th strand. Open out as shown.

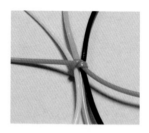

To start, using thumb and index finger to hold, make a horizontal left loop with pink thread and a horizontal right loop with pink thread. Sometimes it is easier to lie your strands on a flat surface when making the first stitch.

Start with the vertical loops. Make a top black loop and a bottom black loop threading over and under as you work.

Continue the same procedure for the remaining two lengths, therefore, make a top green loop and a bottom green loop, a top yellow loop and a bottom yellow loop.

Carefully start to pull all the individual loops quite tightly together. Keep going back to individually tighten each strand into its final place.

If all has worked out correctly you should have a base showing 12 small squares. Think of the 4 squares on the base of the basic square knot! You are doing exactly the same but with 3 strands joined with one horizontal strand.

Repeat the steps until you reach the desired length.

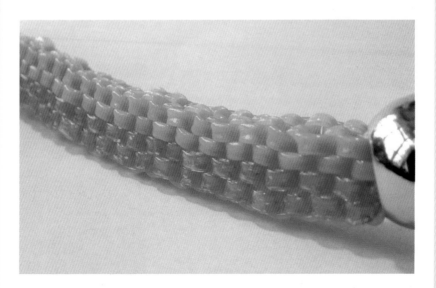

## The 6 Stranded Spiral Scoubi

Definitely one of the more complicated and tricky stitches until you have got the hang of it but, it is well worth the effort as this stitch looks really professional! *Remember all the stitches are worked diagonally.*

There are several ways to start, if you want to make a longer scoubi, you can just tie a knot which you can keep or undo once your scoubi is finished, or temporarily secure with an elastic band. You can start with the knot 3 principle – you just need to work with an extra strand. Or like the picture opposite (bottom) you can start by threading your key ring onto a scoubi and then through a bead. Whichever method you decide:

To start, make a horizontal left loop with white thread to lie on top and a horizontal right loop with white thread to lie below. *(Note: the first horizontal stitch is not diagonal).*

Start with the diagonal vertical loops. Top: Using the darker blue strand, diagonally go over the white strand but through the bottom white loop. Bottom: The dark blue strand goes over the first white loop but under the second white strand.

Continue the same procedure for the remaining two 60 cm lengths, therefore, the pale blue top strand

The pale blue bottom strand is taken over the white loop but under top white strand (through). The last strand is diagonally threaded over top white loop but under (through) the bottom white strand.

Carefully pull all the individual loops quite tightly together, then go back and individually tighten each strand into its final place. If all has worked out correctly you should have a base showing 8 small squares. Have patience — it gets to be as easy as 1,2,3.

### Stitch Two
Is the same basic principle only the white horizontal threads must now also be placed diagonally.

Think of the 4 squares on the base of the basic round knot, you are just working 2 round knotted scoubis side by side.

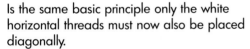

## Angles

To be able to change direction is very useful for many projects. Angles are also very useful when making letters or numbers.

Follow the instructions carefully until you are confident.

Hold the scoubi so that you are looking at the angle you need to make.

Take the back strand and bring it around to the front, underneath the left hand strand (or right if that is the direction you want).

Make a backward loop with the strand brought from the back and a forward loop with the end finishing the opposite way. (The loop goes in front of the scoubi).

Thread the right hand strand through the left hand loop. Thread the left hand thread through the right hand loop.

Pull carefully until you get the shape in the photograph (Stitch positioning should now be back to normal) Continue as required.

# Project Section

## Simple Key Rings

These key rings are great for beginners and can be made very quickly. Anything goes for these projects. The pictures give a few ideas but you can be very creative with key rings and use your own design.

It is easiest to secure your strands onto the key ring with a single looped knot one. A creative alternative uses a bead.

The beads are secured to the ends simply by tying a knot.

You can thread small beads to your project using see through thread whilst working or even sew them on after you have finished.

You could even try using coloured threads to add extra interest.

## Simple Zip Pulls

**You will Need:**

scoubi strands
1cm split ring
beads

A great accessory for your favourite jumper or jacket. The great thing about scoubi's is that they are waterproof so it doesn't matter if they get wet!

Work on the key ring idea but use a very small split ring (1cm) which will fit nicely in the hole on your zip tab.

The pictures give some ideas on what you can do.

## Crazy Hairclip

Very fast and easy to make and lots of fun. Ideal for beginners and a great way to use up all your scraps. The picture is only one idea, a great chance to make your own designs.

Cut all your scoubi scraps into different lengths. Make the coils by threading a piece of wire through the strand, (p10) and wrapping around a pencil.

Put a thick layer of strong glue along the clip and start adding all your bits. Leave the first layer to dry and then you can add another layer. (Too many layers eventually collapse!)

You can also add small beads to your project. Glue them on whilst working or after the clip has dried.

## Crazy Brooch

A great accessory for your favourite jumper or jacket.

Use the same method as the hairclip but use a brooch back instead of the hair clip.

### You will Need:

scoubi scraps
brooch back
wire / scissors
strong glue

## Crazy Magnet

### You will Need:

scoubi scraps
magnet
wire / scissors
strong glue

Follow the instructions for the hairclip but build onto a magnet instead.

## Simple Bracelet

These bracelets are the easiest and fastest makes in the whole book. They are great for beginners and the experienced alike because they are so stylish. The pictures give a few ideas to get you started. Why not experiment and share your results with your friends.

### You will Need:

25cm scoubi strand
beads

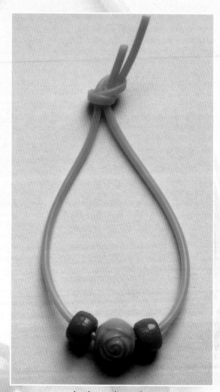

To make these bracelets, cut a scoubi length at least 25 cm. Slide your beads onto the strand and tie to your wrist. Ask a friend to help if it is too difficult to do on your own.

*The lavender section*

## Simple Necklace

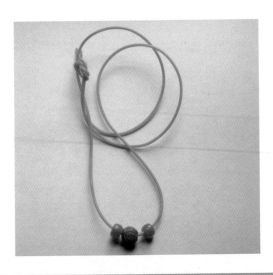

### You will Need:

50cm scoubi strand
beads

A great accessory to match your bracelet.

Use the same method as the bracelet but you need to cut a scoubi length at least 50cm.

## Ring

### You will Need:

scoubi scraps
scissors
strong glue

Cut a length to fit around your finger. Put a spot of glue on both ends and slide your bead on. Make sure that both ends are in evenly. Leave to dry overnight.

## Beaded Bangle

### You will Need:

1 x scoubi strand
wire
beads

These bangles are a little bit different. They are simple to make with great results.

To make these bangles, wrap a scoubi around your wrist as many times as you want. Cut the length you need.

Thread a piece of wire through the scoubi, remember to leave at least 1.5 cm at each end. Thread your beads along the wired scoubi in the design you want. Stop the end beads falling off by folding the end wire over a bead and then twisting. You can hide the twisted wire inside the scoubi.

## Plaited Bookmark

Plaiting with scoubis is very easy.  It is even easier if you are not sat in a very warm place because the strands tend to soften when warm!

Thread all 3 strands onto a pony bead.  They should be secure enough without glue, but you can add a spot of glue to be extra sure! Thread a couple more beads onto one or two strands – you can use your own design but the last one needs to have all 3 strands threaded through to secure the bead.

Plait the strands. Just remember to keep going left over right and then right over left.

When you reach the length you want, again secure the plaiting with one pony bead.

## Wired Necklace and Bracelet

### Necklace

Thread wire through the 55 cm and 50 cm scoubi strands leaving enough at the ends to attach fastenings, (minimum 3cm)

Left side
Thread your beads on to the end and then secure a 7 mm jump ring to the end by folding wire over and twisting. Either trim closely or hide the wire end in the strand.

If you want beads on the scoubi strands thread them now.

Right side
Repeat the same process, remember to thread the beads before attaching the bracelet hook.

### Bracelet

Complete in exactly the same way, the only difference is the length of the scoubi strands. 18 and 19 cm is only a guide. If your wrist is much smaller or much larger adjust the measurements.

Why not complete the set and make some earrings and rings to match. It makes a lovely present.

### Variation

Cut 2 scoubi lengths the same size, reinforce and twist together. You can still add beads to create a great design.

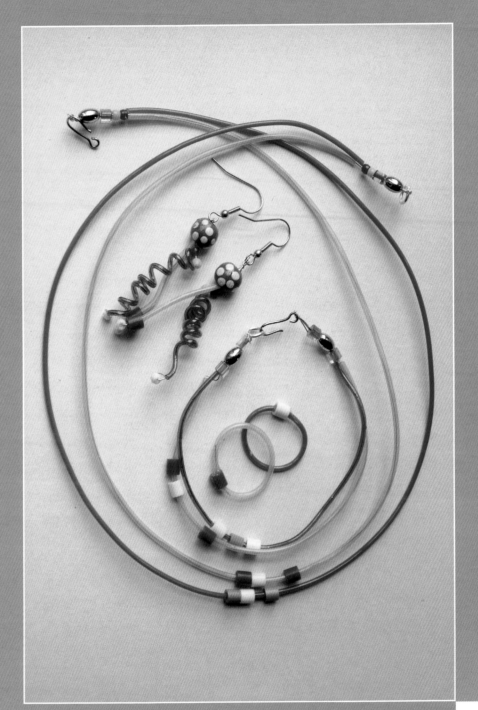

## The Secret Scoubi Code

The easiest way to use scoubidou's is to just make a bracelet or necklace by taking one strand and tying it. You can add a few beads if you want but you can also be part of the secret scoubidou language.

The tables below give you lots of starters:

| Colour combination | Meaning | Colour combination | Meaning |
|---|---|---|---|
| Red | Best friend | Red + white | I'm all yours |
| Blue | I'm sorry | Red + blue | Secret friends |
| Yellow | Lets be friends | Red + yellow | You're the only one |
| Green | Lets make up | Blue + pink | Girl friend |
| White | Friends forever | Blue + purple | Boy friend |
| Black | Lets hang out | Red + orange | Together forever |
| Orange | Groovy Gal | Orange + white | Heart broken |
| Pink | Babe | Orange + yellow | It will never end |
| Purple | Fab friends | Pink + pink | Beautiful eyes |
| White + White | 100% Angel | Pink and black | You're my teddy bear |
| Black + Black | 100% Devil | Blue + black | Muscle man |
| Red + yellow | It's a girl thing | Purple + white | Brain box |
| Blue + yellow | Your secret's safe | Yellow and yellow | Cheeky monkey |
| Blue + green | All girl team | Yellow + blue | Daft as a brush |
| Blue + white | Girls together | Green + black | Bees knees |
| Purple + black | Don't stop | Pink + white | Soul Mate |

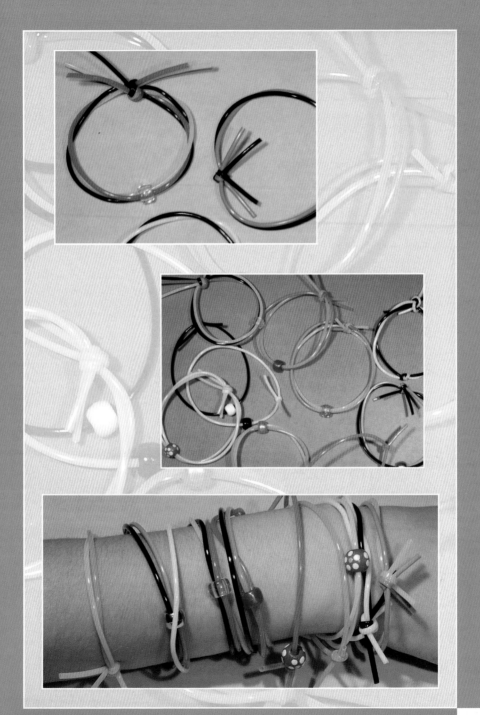

## Simple Key Ring

### You will Need:

scoubi strands
key ring holder
trimmings

These key rings are great for beginners and can be made very quickly.

First, choose which start knot you are going to use, if you use knot 1 or 2 you can attach your key ring to the centre of the strands before you tie your knot. If you choose to start with knot 3 then you can be very clever and incorporate the key ring on the starting knot or, you can attach it later.

The most difficult thing to decide is what stitch to use. All knots work well for key rings. Follow the step by step instructions from the Skills section after you have made your choice and knot to what ever length you choose.

You can be very creative with key rings and make your own designs. Add beads to the ends and secure simply by tying a knot at the end. You can thread small beads to your project using see through thread whilst working or even sew them on after you have finished. You could even try using coloured threads to add extra interest.

# PROJECT 13

## Bicycle Ties

Take any of these ideas and tie them to your bike with a spare scoubi scrap. Without the key ring of course. The bells are fun because they tinkle when you ride.

The green section

## Octopus

A real favourite which is very quick and easy to make. It can sit on your desk or you can make it into a key ring. They are so quick to make that you could make a whole colony!

Find the centres of the two strands and cut in half. Working with double strands throughout, start with knot 3, try to attach the key ring now.

Continue using square stitch for about 3 cm. Pull the last stitch tightly making sure that you have left threads at least 5cm long to tie your beads to.

Tie beads on the end of the 8 strands. You will usually have to tie double knots to make sure the beads to not slip off.

Glue the eyes to your octopus and trim the ends.

### You will Need:

2 x 1m scoubis
pair of 5mm eyes
8 pony beads
1 key ring
scissors
glue

# Face Magnet

This is only one idea but you can be really creative and easily make your own designs.

Measure 10 cm and tie an elastic band around the strands at this point. Start to work in what ever stitch you choose. The picture uses round stitch.

**You will Need:**

2 x 1m scoubi strands
2 x eyes
wire
cocktail stick
scoubi scrap
scissors

Continue until you have 10 cm left at the end. Take a piece of wire about 4 cm long and lay over the last stitch, work one more stitch to secure. Untie the elastic band and thread wire under the first stitch. Go back and tie this stitch tightly. Tie the two ends together to make a round shape. Cut enough wire lengths to fit into all end strands. Use your cocktail stick to coil the strands to make hair.

Take your scoubi scrap and tie 2 loose knots to make glasses frame. Remember to leave ends long enough to glue the frames to the face. Glue eyes onto loose knots and glue the glasses onto the face.

Glue the magnet onto the back.

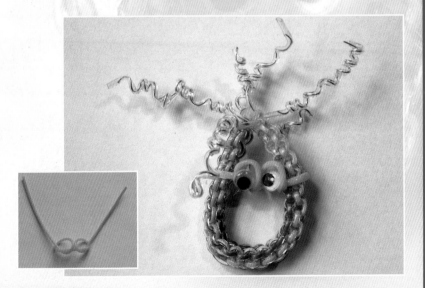

## Mouse Magnet

Very cute and fun to make.

Start using knot 3 and reinforce your scoubi. Continue with the 4 stranded scoubi (see page 18) stitch until you have used all the strands. Pull the last stitch tightly. Remember to keep the wire hidden in the centre.

Bend the scoubi into shape and secure using the end wires.  Trim both the scoubi strands and wire closely.

Cut out 2 ears in grey and 2 smaller ears in pink felt.  Also cut out one small pink nose.

Use scoubi scraps cut in half for whiskers and glue first.   Add the nose and ears and eyes. Finally, glue the magnet on the back and leave to dry.

# PROJECT 17

## Black Cat Brooch

Work in exactly the same way as the mouse but use black scoubi's and cut 2 x cat ears. Use a brooch back.

The green section

# Templates

Cut 1
nose

Cut 2
grey ears

Cut 2
pink
ears

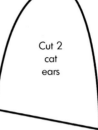

Cut 2
cat
ears

# Knotted Bracelets

Scoubi bracelets and jewellery are very quick and easy to make. They can be as simple or as complicated as you choose.

Start using knot 1 tied loosely because when you have finished you will be unpicking it. (If you prefer you can secure the ends with an elastic band).

Continue with any stitch. Stop when you have knotted the length you require. You can test how long to make your bracelet by wrapping it around your wrist whilst working and adding at least 6 stitches so that it will slip over your hand. Make sure you have at least 3 cm of strands left before you pull your last stitch tightly.

Carefully unpick your starting knot or remove the elastic band. Thread two strands from each end of the bracelet into the pony bead. Tie these four strands together securely. It is easier to tie only two strands together at once, this makes two knots but they are not easily noticed. Repeat this step for the remaining 4 strands.

Trim the ends neatly - preferably the next day.

If you make a very loose round stitch you get a completely different effect – almost lacy.

**TIP**
If you find it difficult to thread 4 strands through one bead you can add an extra bead. Make sure that you thread at least one strand from each side through the bead.

## Knotted Bracelets with Fastenings

### You will Need:

4 x 1m scoubis
bracelet fastenings
(jump rings and
clasps)
wire, pliers
scissors

Scoubis are very versatile. If you want a more professional look make your bracelet using fastenings. Fastenings are very useful for necklaces also.

To start, tie a loose knot (you will be unpicking it once you have finished your knotting) and choose a stitch!

Continue until you have knotted your required length. Test the length as you are progressing by wrapping around your wrist.

Thread a piece of wire about 4 cm long under the last stitch and twist a couple of times to secure. Complete two more stitches over the wire. Attach your fastenings to the wire. Fold the wire over and hide through the centre of the bracelet. Twist the ends until secure. (Make sure you do not twist too much and snap the wire).

Unpick the start knot and repeat the last step making sure the first stitch is tight.

## TIPS

If you do not want to use wire, you can simply incorporate a hook whilst making your starting knot. You can then attatch the jump ring at the opposite end with the last of the scoubi strands tied in a knot. This is not quite so tidy but works well.

## Plaited Bracelet and Necklace

### You will Need:

bracelet
3 x 1m scoubis
bracelet fastenings
(jump rings and
clasps/hooks)
scissors

### Bracelet

Take 2 scoubis and tie them together as close to the top as you can. Tie very tightly to make the joining knot as small as posible. Then, take the last strand and fold it in half to find the centre. It is neater to slide your hook fastening on at this stage.

Continue with plait stitch until you reach the length you need. Finish by tying the two outside strands together on the back.

Attach your jump ring simply by tying on. Trim all ends closely to make neat.

### You will Need:

necklace
5 x 1m scoubis
necklace fastenings
(jump rings and
clasps/hooks)
scissors

### Necklace

The necklace is made in exactly the same way as the bracelet. However, you will need to join in two more outer strands for the extra length.

Work until you have only 3 cm left of your outside strands. Tie the remaining two outside strands in a tight knot and join onto the middle strands by tying another knot. Make sure that the joining knot is on the back of your work. Make your next stitch using the existing outside strands working them over the new strands. Tie the old strands in a knot on the back of your work and continue in exactly the same way using the new strands.

The green section

## VARIATIONS

The plait stitch can be tied very tightly to give one effect but by leaving the knots loose you will  get a totally different look. The looser look is easier to set and thread beads into.

## Triangular Bracelet and Necklace

This bracelet is very simple to make and is very effective.

First, take your three strands and fold them in half to find the centre. Then slide a bead through all three strands to the centre point.

Make two triangular stitches on one side and then two on the opposite side to stop the bead from moving.

Work in triangular stitch on both sides until you have knotted enough to fit your wrist. Remember to add several stitches so as the bracelet will fit over your hand.

Thread two strands from one side and one from the other onto a bead. Do the same with the remaining three strands. Tie knots to stop the bead falling off. Carefully trim the ends.

### You will Need:

**bracelet**
3 x 1m scoubis
1 x pony bead
fastenings
strong glue, wire
scissors

### You will Need:

**necklace**
6 x 1m scoubis
3 x pony beads
fastenings
strong glue, wire
scissors

### Variation

When you are more proficient, you can join the both ends together invisibly by meshing the two ends together basically using a variation of the 6 stranded scoubi technique.

# Necklace

The necklace is a little more tricky because you need to join 2 lengths of scoubis.

To start, take 3 strands and tie a knot at one end. Work in triangular stitch until you have only 4-5cm left. Pull the last stitch tightly. Repeat this step with the remaining 3 strands for the other side.

Measure your beads and cut each end of the scoubi strands leaving half this amount (therefore, 3 pony beads measure approx 2 cm, so you need to trim the strands leaving 1 cm on both pieces). Thread a 5 cm piece of wire through the three beads to add extra strength. Put a spot of strong glue on both ends and slide the beads over. Secure by twisting the wire around the knotted ends. Leave to dry completely.

Untie knots and thread a piece of wire approx 4 cm long under the last stitch at each end, twist to secure. Work two more stitches and attach the fastenings.

## Earrings

### You will Need:

Scoubi scraps
beads
earring fastenings
wire, pliers
scissors
pencil/skewer

Scoubi earrings are straightforward and quick to make, they are also fun to wear. The variations are endless, you can have earrings to match all your favourite outfits and it is a great way to use your end scraps.

Start by threading a wire through your strand. Remember to leave some wire (minimum 2 cm) at the top end for beads and fastenings.

Wind the strand around the pencil, or if you prefer something thinner, a cocktail stick. Carefully slide off your pencil.

Thread beads onto the tops and attach your fastenings. You need to twist the wire to secure the earrings to the hooks. Trim wires.

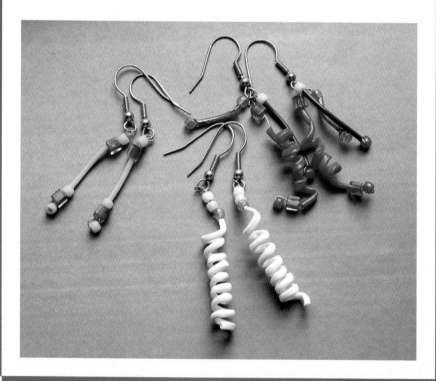

## Spiral Earrings

Cut 2 x 100 cm scoubi lengths in half.
You should now have 4 halves – 2 for each
earring.

Take the third strand and cut in half. Fold the
first piece in half and slide your earring to
the central point before continuing.

Start the spiral stitch using Knot 2 and continue until you reach the length
you require.  As a guide, the photograph uses about 20 stitches.

Put a spot of glue on the spiral ends when trimming closely.

Attach earring fastenings.

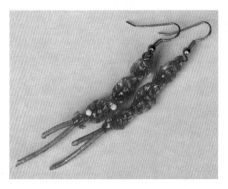

## Hairclips

### You will Need:

1 x hair clip
3 x scoubis (single)
5 x scoubis (double)
glue
scissors
(wire)

Make a hair clip to match jewellery you have already made with scoubis.

These hairclips also make lovely gifts.

The pictures show hairclips using both one and two outside strands. One strand gives a thinner appearance.

Start using knot 2 and the plait stitch. If you are using double threads, slide the second outside strand under the first before firmly securing the knot.

Continue until you have made a scoubi the length of the hairclip plus 1 cm and finish by tying a knot on the back of your work.

Trim very closely to the ends of the middle strands. Leave enough space so as the stitches do not slip off and add a spot of strong clear glue to make sure your ends are secure.

Glue onto the clip and leave to dry.

### TIP
It is useful to wrap wire/thread around both the scoubi and clip to 'train' the scoubi to lie flat against the clip whilst drying.

## Variations

Add beads to your creation. Either sew on after you have finished your scoubi (but before you glue it to the clip) or weave beads into the scoubi whilst working by using see through thread.

## Christmas Novelties

For the characters you need to start with a basic shape which is made from 2 x 100 cm strands, in any stitch, but they need to be reinforced. Fold in half and secure with a small piece of wire on the back. Continue by following the individual instructions.

**Project 25 Angel -** You will also need: 1½ glitter pipe cleaners, 1 x small paper head.

Make the basic shape. Cut 4 pieces of pipe cleaner 3 cm long and shape 2 into circles for feet and 2 into smaller circles for hands. Cut another length 7 cm long and shape for a halo with a wire coming down. Glue onto head. Shape a whole pipe cleaner into wings.

Assemble all pieces and glue onto your angel. Use a felt tip pen to draw eyes and a mouth on the paper ball.

**Project 26 Father Christmas -** You will also need: red and black felt, 1 x small and medium pom pom, 2 eyes.

Start with a basic shape. Cut out a red felt hat. Glue the hat down the back seam and then glue on the pom pom. Cut 2 hands and feet in black felt and glue them onto the basic shape. Glue the head into the hat and then glue eyes. Glue the head onto the body.

Leave to dry.

## Project 27 Angel 2

Start with a basic reinforced triangular shape. Then continue using the same instructions for the angels in project 25. Secure the ends at the top and bend into the shape you need.

## Project 28 Bell

Start with a basic triangular shape. Then thread wire through the green scoubi and bend into shape to form leaves. Secure together by twisting the wire. Add the red beads for berries and the bell. If you want to hang it on your Christmas tree, make an extra wire loop whilst making leaves.

Project 26
Father Christmas -
Red felt hat
template.

## Pipe Cleaner Man

### You will Need:

2 x scoubis
1 x pipe cleaner
4 x pony beads
2 x eyes
1 x small seed bead
1 x medium pom pom
glue, scissors

Start with knot 3 and work one complete stitch. Then cut a 10 cm length of pipe cleaner for legs. Find the centre and rest pipe cleaner on top of the bottom stitch.

Holding the legs in place, work another square stitch over the pipe cleaner. *Pull this stitch tightly to secure the legs into position.

Continue in square stitch for 3cm (about 18 stitches) to form the body. Cut a pipe cleaner 8 cm long for the arms and work in exactly the same way as the legs.

Complete 3 more stitches. Put a drop of glue on the ends of the arms and legs and slide on pony beads. Glue the head onto the body. Add eyes and a tiny pink bead for a nose.

The green section

## Spring Man

Cut 2 x 50 cm scoubis. Reinforce both strands with wire. Fold in half to find their centres and wrap each half around a pencil. Carefully slide off taking care not to pull your coils out of shape.

To continue, follow the instructions for project 29 and treat the springs like the pipe cleaner.

Add his scarf, arrange around his neck and glue into place after the head has dried.

Glue on a few coiled scoubi scraps for hair.

### You will Need:

3 x scoubis
1 x paper ball
wire
pipe cleaner scrap
2 x eyes
1 x pink seed bead
glue
scissors

## Key ring / zip pull man

This man uses the same principle as project 29 but you start from the top and work down. (You also do not need a pom pom and eyes). Start with a double looped knot 2. Work one stitch and add pipe cleaner. Work 3 cm and add the legs. Work 2 more stitches. Pull last stitch very tightly. Glue on beads for hands and feet.

## Bride

Take 8 scoubis and hold them together so as they are all the same length. Measure 25 cm and tie an elastic band at this point.

Work an 8 stranded round scoubi for 4 cm (see instructions for 6 stranded scoubi page 16 use same technique, just add 2 more strands).

Divide the strands in half to form legs. Make each leg 3 cm long in a 4 stranded scoubi stitch. It helps to work in the direction you want the legs to lie. Tie the last stitch tightly to end there or, if you prefer, add feet.

To add feet, make a 90 degree angle and then work a further 2 stitches. Pull tightly and trim closely. Leave overnight to 'set' before trimming.

Go back to the top and remove the elastic band. Again, split the 8 strands in half to form arms. Work in exactly the same way as for the legs.

Glue on the head and leave to dry securely. Make skirt and glue onto the body, also cut a strip for veil. Decorate as you wish.

### You will Need:

8 x scoubis
elastic band, felt tips
paper ball (head)
net scraps, beads
stars, glue, scissors

## Yellow Man

Work in exactly the same way as for the bride, project 32, until the figure is complete. Glue pom poms on for hands and head and finally glue on his eyes.

If you prefer you can use pom poms for feet instead of knotting them or leaving them plain.

The green section

## Blue Man

Take 2 strands and fold in half. Start with
Knot 3. Work 2 more square stitches.

Take 2 more strands, fold in half and cut. Lay
these 4 strands over the square stitches
already worked and then continue to make
another stitch over the top (See project 29 for
method). If you do not pull the stitch very
tightly you can make the man sit down when you have finished. Work in
square stitch for a further 2cm.

(See project 29 for method)

Return to the legs and work square stitch on each side for another 2cm.

Back to the top! Fold and cut 2 more strands and lay them over the last
stitch for the body. Work 1 more stitch over these strands.

Go back to the arms, work in
exactly the same way as the legs.
It helps if you can work the arms
in the direction you want them to
go.

Finish with the completion knot
(page 9) to give the effect of hands.

(page 9)

Glue the head onto the body
and the eyes onto the head.

Leave to dry.

> **You will Need:**
> 6 x scoubis
> 1 x medium pom pom
> 2 x eyes
> glue
> scissors

## Caterpillar

This cute caterpillar is very easy to make and looks great. Start with 2 strands and knot 3. Work two stitches.

Cut your 3rd strand into 25 cm lengths and reinforce by threading wire through.

Take your 1st reinforced strand and lay it over the base of the body. Work over the strand to secure the first pair of legs. Work 6 more stitches and repeat the last stage. Do this for the remaining two pairs of legs.

Work 4 more stitches and pull the last stitch tightly. Put a spot of glue on the end. Leave to dry and then cut the bottom two strands. You need the two top strands for antennae.

Cut two pieces of wire 2 cm longer than your antennae and twist a bead onto the top of each one. Twist to secure. Reinforce the antennae with these strands. Go back and glue small pom poms onto the ends of the leg and then the head onto the body. Glue eyes.

## Snail Brooch

Start with dark green strands and knot 3. Work in square stitch for about 5 cm and finish with a completion knot. Cut off the two bottom strands close to the knot. Cut 2 pieces of wire about 4 cm and attach a seed bead to one end of each. Twist securely into place and thread through the two strands, you can hide the twisted ends inside the strand.

**You will Need:**
2 x dark green scoubi strands
2 x pale green scoubi strands
2 x seed beads
brooch back
wire
scissors

With the pale green strands, start with knot 3 and reinforce. Continue in round stitch until you have used all your strands. Roll into a snail shell shape and attach to the body with wire.

Glue to the brooch back.

## Ginger Cat

This cute cat looks great as a fridge magnet or even a brooch.

Start with 4 strands and a knot 1. Work in round stitch until you have about 5 cm of ends left. Lie a 4 cm piece of wire over the last stitch and work 2 more stitches.

Back to the top, unpick the knot and repeat the last stage. You can then join your two ends together in a sort of oval shape by twisting the wire ends together. Make sure that you twist enough before trimming the ends but not so much that the wire snaps.

Cut 2 pieces of pipe cleaner about 4 cm long and bend in half to make ears and glue to one of the pom poms. Add eyes, nose and whiskers. (You can use your trimmings from the scoubi strands, just cut them in half).

Twist a length of pipe cleaner for the tail and glue that to the body and lastly glue the feet.

## Scoubi Pens

These are very 'chic' accessories which every pencil case needs. Definitely something that everyone will want!

They are a little tricky to get started but well worth the effort.

For a long pen, you will need the whole 100 cm length so, the start knot is often the first stitch and needs extra care.

To start, tie a loose knot 1.

Once you have your knot slip the pen inner into the middle of the knot, hold all the ends and pull very tightly.

You have to try and ignore the ends that are sticking out until you have finished and then you can cut them off to make a neat finish.

Continue working with your chosen stitch around the pen inner, remember to pull the stitches quite tight to support the pen. When you have knotted all the way along the inner, make one extra stitch to cover the end of the pen and tie very tightly.

### You will Need:

4 x scoubis
1 x pen inner
scissors
glue
*optional* pony beads

The green section

If you want to be very clever, you can add beads into the project as you work which gives a very professional and 'chic' effect.

Simply slip a bead onto the pen inner and make the next stich on top of the bead.

Return to the start knot, untie, and make sure that the first stitch is pulled tightly. Leave to 'set' overnight before trimming closely to the tip.

If your strands have moved up whilst working, you may need to add a couple of stitches to reach the pen nib.

### TIP / VARIATION
If you struggle with the starting point, try and use a small inner. This will then only need 2 x 1m scoubis and you can start using knot 3.

## Bag Friends

These characters are great fun to make and use. They can keep you company all day!

They are as simple or as complicated as you want to make them, the choice is yours. Here are just a few ideas to get you started but really, this project is a fantastic creative opportunity for you to make your own designs! Browse through the book for more ideas which you can adapt.

Start with the variation of knot 2, where you just make one single loop. This will be the loop where you thread a scoubi scrap (at least 12 cm long) to attach to your bag.

Use the whole length of scoubi strands in any stitch you choose, round, square or spiral work well, until you have just 3 cm of strands left. Pull the last stitch tightly. Shape into a circle and either secure with a small piece of wire leaving the top loop free or simply tie the scoubi strand around the loop at the bottom tightly.

Now the fun begins, you can add eyes, ears, nose and mouth, glasses and bow ties. Make an alien from outer space or a Father Christmas.

The butterfly's body is made using spiral stitch. The wings are made with a 38 cm scoubi which has been reinforced so as you can make the wing shape.

### You will Need:

2 x 100cm scoubi strands
scissors
wire, strong glue

### Accessories:

pom poms
eyes
felt scraps,
ribbon
beads